THE
POCKET

The
Beatles

Published in 2026
by Gemini Gift Books
Part of Gemini Books Group

Based in Woodbridge and London

Marine House, Tide Mill Way,
Woodbridge, Suffolk IP12 1AP
United Kingdom

www.geminibooks.com

Text and Design © 2026 Gemini Gift Books Ltd
Part of the Gemini Pockets series

Cover illustration by Natalie Foss

ISBN 978-1-80247-325-4

Manufacturer's EU Representative: Eurolink Compliance Limited,
25 Herbert Place, Dublin, D02 AY86, Republic of Ireland.
admin@eurolink-europe.ie

Printed in China

10 9 8 7 6 5 4 3 2 1

Picture Credits: 4: Alamy/Retro AdArchives;
7: Alamy/Associated Press; 8: Alamy/L.T. Myers;
38: Alamy/PictureLux, The Hollywood Archive;
68: Alamy/Smith Archive; 98: Alamy/Peter

THE
POCKET

The
Beatles

G:

BEATLEMANIA

ASTORIA THEATRE

CONTENTS

Introduction

Roll up! Roll up for the mystery tour!

From their early days catching buses at Penny Lane to performing on the rooftops of London's Savile Row, the mop tops' ten-year tenure at the top of the charts is unlike any rags-to-riches tale you've heard before, and is likely never to be seen again. With John, Paul, George and Ringo as our guides, we shall walk the long and winding road, exploring the band's greatest hits, the moments that incited the most mania and the key ingredients that make these Beatles (with an A) so magical. This tiny tome is a timeless celebration of their achievements and their enduring legacy, as well as a daily reminder to us all to let peace, love and understanding into our lives at all times. So, ladies and gentlemen, let me introduce you to the one and only... the Beatles.

Come on in...

Chapter One

Beatles
with an A

\\ **Once upon a time there were three little boys called John, George and Paul. They decided to get together because they were the getting together type. When they were together they wondered what for after all, what for? So all of a sudden they grew guitars and fashioned a noise.** \\

John Lennon, *Mersey Beat*, July 1961

6 July 1957

It was on this magical day at St. Peter's Church fête in Woolton, Liverpool, that John Lennon met his "first true love", Paul McCartney. A year earlier, Lennon had formed the skiffle group called the Quarrymen*. After their performance that day at the fête, he invited McCartney to join. "I knew the words to 25 rock songs, so I got in the group," McCartney said. "'Long Tall Sally' and 'Tutti-Frutti', that got me in. That was my audition."

It was McCartney who would later introduce his friend George Harrison to Lennon on 6 February 1958.

* Named after Lennon's former Liverpudlian school, Quarry Bank.

The Beatles #1: John Lennon

John Lennon was the founder and leader of the Beatles from 1958 until manager Brian Epstein's untimely passing in 1967. Famed for his sharp and sarcastic wit and intellect, Lennon was an outspoken advocate for peace in his post-Beatles career, alongside his second wife Yoko Ono. His biggest hit outside of the Beatles was 'Imagine', released in October 1971. In 1975, Lennon told *Rolling Stone*: "I've got used to the fact – just about – that whatever I do is going to be compared to the other Beatles. If I took up ballet dancing, my ballet dancing would be compared with Paul McCartney's bowling."

7 August 1957

The date the Quarrymen (pre-Beatles) first played at Liverpool's Cavern Club, primarily a jazz and skiffle venue. The other acts on the bill were Ron McKay's Skiffle Group, Dark Town Skiffle Group and The Deltones Skiffle Group. The group played a selection of rock and roll covers, including Elvis Presley's 'Hound Dog' and 'Blue Suede Shoes'. While on stage, Lennon received a note from the club's owner with a request: "Cut out the bloody rock 'n' roll!"

From Bugs to Beat

Before settling on the iconic "Beatles", the band cycled through names such as the Black Jacks, Quarrymen, Rainbows, Silver Beatles, Beatals and Johnny and the Moondogs. They first performed as "the Beatles" on 15 August 1960, at The Jacaranda club in Liverpool. The name is often credited to Stuart Sutcliffe, John Lennon's art school friend and the band's original bassist, drawing inspiration from Buddy Holly's Crickets.

❯❯ How did the name arrive? It came in a vision – a man appeared in a flaming pie and said unto them 'From this day on you are Beatles with an A.' 'Thank you, Mister Man,' they said, thanking him. ❯❯

John Lennon, *Mersey Beat*, 1964

21 February 1961

The day the Beatles played their first show –
of 292! – at the Cavern Club, a beloved music
venue at 10 Mathew Street in the heart of
Liverpool city. It was here that they were spotted
by manager Brian Epstein in November 1961.
At the time, Pete Best was the drummer of the
group, and the band was paid £6 for its
performance – about £65 today. "Liverpool!
Cavern! These are words that go together well!"
McCartney exclaimed when he returned to
the club in June 2018.

Bass Beatle

Lennon's original Quarrymen bassist (from 1957–1961), Stuart Sutcliffe, died in Hamburg at just 21 – the official cause of death was a cerebral haemorrhage. Paul McCartney reluctantly took over Stuart's duties in July 1961, the first of many major milestones for the group's musical evolution.

"None of us wanted to be the bass player," Paul McCartney told *Bass Player* magazine in July 1995. "It wasn't the number one job: we wanted to be up front. In our minds, it was the fat guy in the group who played the bass, and he stood at the back. None of us wanted that; we wanted to be up front singing, looking good, to pull the birds."

Today, McCartney is considered one of the most influential, and iconic, bass players in rock history.

"There are only four people who knew what the Beatles were about."

Paul McCartney, *Playboy*, December 1984

Beatles on Repeat

Between August 1960 and December 1962,
the Beatles travelled to Hamburg, Germany,
five times and played more than 250 shows.
Their booking agent, Allan Williams, knew
that the city's Reeperbahn nightclubs offered
bands regular gigs and better pay than
those in Liverpool. These often-gruelling
performances – including a three-month
residency at the Top Ten Club in 1961 where
they played 92 consecutive nights! – sometimes
lasted eight hours a night, with only a fifteen-
minute break every hour. This intense schedule
was crucial in strengthening their stagecraft
and musical stamina.

"Hamburg wrecked us," Paul McCartney
recalled in *The Beatles Anthology*, 1995.
"I remember getting home and my dad thought
I was half-dead. I looked like a skeleton, I hadn't
noticed the change, I'd been having such a ball."

'My Bonnie'

In June 1961, the Beatles recorded 'My Bonnie' with British rocker Tony Sheridan on lead vocals – a track that was not considered part of their official canon. The single was credited to "The Beatles and Tony Sheridan", with the band serving as Sheridan's backing group.

When it was first released in Germany in October 1961, the Beatles were renamed "The Beat Brothers". The reason? In German schoolyard slang, "Beatles" sounded uncomfortably close to "peedles" – which meant, well, a penis.

During their Hamburg club days, the Beatles found the pun hilarious, often jokingly referring to themselves as "Beatle Peedles".

Merseybeat

As the Beatles rose in popularity in 1963, so too did the defining genre of music they played – Merseybeat. It was the first time in British pop music history that a sound and a location were linked together. Developed around Liverpool, or more specifically the River Mersey, in the late 1950s and early 1960s, Merseybeat melded influences from British and American rock and roll, rhythm and blues, skiffle, traditional pop and music hall – all united by a relentless 4/4 back beat.

The Fab Four

The Beatles may have been nicknamed the "Fab Four", but, individually, they had unique personalities and characters. This distinctiveness was a blessing for their music but a curse on their longevity. It's often been said that all the girls swooned for Paul, all the boys wanted to be John but were secretly George, and Ringo was the one you could take home to meet your mum. They were even given nicknames by the press:

The Cute One: Paul McCartney
The Smart One: John Lennon
The Quiet One: George Harrison
The Funny One: Ringo Starr

Essential Album #1:
Please Please Me

1. 'I Saw Her Standing There'
2. 'Misery'
3. 'Anna (Go to Him)'
4. 'Chains'
5. 'Boys'
6. 'Ask Me Why'
7. 'Please Please Me'
8. 'Love Me Do'
9. 'P.S. I Love You'
10. 'Baby It's You'
11. 'Do You Want to Know a Secret'
12. 'A Taste of Honey'
13. 'There's a Place'
14. 'Twist and Shout'

The Beatles' debut album, *Please Please Me*, was released in the UK on 22 March 1963. All 14 tracks – including eight McCartney–Lennon compositions – were recorded in a single ten-hour session on 11 February 1963 at Abbey Road Studios. Each band member was paid approximately £7.50 (around £200 today) for their work. The final song recorded was 'Twist and Shout' – now one of the group's most iconic tracks – captured in a single take! The album topped the UK charts in May 1963 for 30 weeks before being succeeded by their second album, *With the Beatles*.

From Record Stores to Recording Albums

After witnessing the Beatles perform at the Cavern Club on 9 November 1961, Brian Epstein, a local record store manager, agreed to manage the band after his store began to receive requests for their German-recorded single 'My Bonnie'. Despite having no prior experience managing a band, it was Epstein who secured an audition with George Martin – the "fifth Beatle" – a producer at EMI's Parlophone label, in May 1962.

❝ **The Beatles are the best, and I say to you here in 1965, that the children of the twenty-first century will be listening to them.** ❞

Brian Epstein, Larry Kane interview, 1965

Essential Album #2

With the Beatles

1. 'It Won't Be Long'
2. 'All I've Got to Do'
3. 'All My Loving'
4. 'Don't Bother Me'
5. 'Little Child'
6. 'Till There Was You'
7. 'Please Mister Postman'
8. 'Roll Over Beethoven'
9. 'Hold Me Tight'
10. 'You Really Got a Hold on Me'
11. 'I Wanna Be Your Man'
12. 'Devil in Her Heart'
13. 'Not a Second Time'
14. 'Money (That's What I Want)'

Released just eight months after their debut album, *With the Beatles* arrived on 22 November 1963 and catapulted the group to global fame. Remarkably, it held the UK's No. 1 album spot for 21 weeks – succeeding their first album – giving them an extraordinary 51 consecutive weeks at the top.

A standout track, 'All My Loving', opened their legendary *Ed Sullivan Show* debut on 9 February 1964 and was praised by Lennon as "a damn good piece of work". Interestingly, it was the first McCartney song in which the lyrics came before the music – a process he considered his first foray into poetry.

Mop Top

When Brian Epstein took over as the Beatles' manager in late 1961, his first priority was refining their image. Wanting to broaden their appeal beyond the leather-clad "Teddy Boy" aesthetic, he insisted the band wear matching, tailored suits – often made of mohair – and encouraged them to abandon their slicked-back hairstyles in favour of what would become the iconic "mop-top" – a style that looked like, well, like a mop! It was a clean-cut yet subtly rebellious look that Epstein believed would make them more palatable to record labels and mainstream audiences.

Reflecting on this transformation in a 2011 *Radio Times* interview, McCartney said: "It was the simplest of ideas, but it suddenly made us one person – a four-headed monster!"

Big Blunder

With a now-infamous remark, Decca Records executive Dick Rowe rejected the Beatles in 1962 after hearing them perform 15 tracks at a lunch meeting – a decision widely regarded as one of the greatest blunders in music history. Speaking directly to their manager Brian Epstein, Rowe dismissed the band, saying "Not to mince words, Mr Epstein, we don't like your boys' sound. Groups of four guitarists are on their way out."

In response, Epstein reportedly fired back: "You must be out of your mind! These boys are going to explode. I am completely confident that one day they will be bigger than Elvis Presley."

Of course, Epstein's prediction came true. After signing with EMI, the Beatles went on to became global superstars – and Rowe, seeking redemption, later signed another soon-to-be-legendary band: the Rolling Stones.

The Ed Sullivan Show

In 1963, as the Beatles returned to London from a show in Sweden, they were greeted by hundreds of screaming fans at Heathrow airport. Among the onlookers was American television host Ed Sullivan, who was fascinated by the chaos. Sensing something big, he swiftly made plans to book the band for his popular television programme.

That decision led to the Beatles' iconic appearance on *The Ed Sullivan Show* on 9 February 1964. Watched by more than 73 million viewers, it marked their explosive breakthrough in America and transformed the landscape of popular music. As Sullivan later recalled, "I have never seen any scenes to compare with the bedlam that was occasioned by their debut … Broadway was jammed with people for almost eight blocks. They screamed, yelled, and stopped traffic. It was indescribable … There has never been anything like it in show business!"

Pop Pioneers

The Beatles were pioneers in music, fashion and culture and were the first to elevate pop music to serious artistic expression. During their eight-year reign, the mop tops achieved numerous firsts for a band:

First to:
- Use guitar feedback ('I Feel Fine')
- Start a song with a fade-in ('Eight Days a Week')
- Use backwards tape loops and reverse sounds ('Rain')
- Use a sitar in a pop recording
- Release an album without the band name on the cover (*Sgt. Pepper*)
- Popularize the concept album (*Sgt. Pepper*)
- Stage a concert (as an entertainment act) in a sports stadium (Shea Stadium)
- Publicly renounce touring at their commercial peak
- Have a simultaneous No. 1 single and album in both the US and the UK

Wimbledon's Palais Setlist

1. 'I Saw Her Standing There'

2. 'From Me to You'

3. 'All My Loving'

4. 'You've Really Got a Hold on Me'

5. 'Roll Over Beethoven'

6. 'Boys'

7. 'Till There Was You'

8. 'She Loves You'

9. 'Money (That's What I Want)'

10. 'Twist and Shout'

On 14 December 1963, the Beatles performed a special concert for 3,000 ecstatic fans. Arriving onstage at 3:30 PM, the band powered through ten songs while fans surged toward them. Fearing a stage rush, the Palais management built a raised platform surrounded by a steel cage to hold back the crowd. As the front rows crushed against the barrier, John Lennon hilariously yelled, "If they press any harder, they'll come through as chips!"

After the show, the band greeted fans behind the bar – several fainted on the spot. Beatlemania had officially arrived!

Essential Album #3
A Hard Day's Night

1. 'A Hard Day's Night'
2. 'I Should Have Known Better'
3. 'If I Fell'
4. 'I'm Happy Just to Dance with You'
5. 'And I Love Her'
6. 'Tell Me Why'
7. 'Can't Buy Me Love'
8. 'Any Time at All'
9. 'I'll Cry Instead'
10. 'Things We Said Today'
11. 'When I Get Home'
12. 'You Can't Do That'
13. 'I'll Be Back'

Released on 10 June 1964, *A Hard Day's Night* marked a major milestone for the Beatles: it was their first album to feature only original material – and the only one composed entirely of Lennon–McCartney songs. Among its standout tracks is 'Can't Buy Me Love', one of the band's earliest major hits. It was notable for several reasons – it was the first Beatles song to open with its chorus, the first to feature a single lead vocal (Paul) without their trademark harmonies and was a defining example of the band's pop innovation.

Years later, in 1966, McCartney shared a memory about the song during his first trip to the US as a superstar: "I remember meeting this rather nice girl and taking her out for dinner in this MG in the cool Florida night, palm trees swaying. A Liverpool boy with this tanned beauty in my MG going out to dinner. The song should have been called '*Can* Buy Me Love', actually."

\\ Paul provided a lightness, an optimism, while I would always go for the sadness, the discords, the bluesy notes. There was a period when I thought I didn't write melodies, that Paul wrote those and I just wrote straight, shouting rock 'n' roll. But when I think of some of my own songs, I was writing melody with the best of them. \\

John Lennon, *Playboy*, September 1980

The Power of Nine

The number nine held notable significance
for the Beatles, particularly John Lennon.
Born on 9 October, Lennon's connection to
the number appears throughout key moments:

• Brian Epstein first saw the band on 9
November 1961, securing their EMI contract
on 9 May 1962

• Lennon met Yoko Ono on 9 November 1966
and penned three songs with the number nine
in their titles: 'Revolution 9', '#9 Dream' and
'One After 909' (written at 9 Newcastle Road)

• Tragically, after being shot, Lennon was
taken to Roosevelt Hospital on Ninth Avenue
and pronounced dead at 11:07 pm
(1+1+0+7=9) – spooky

Chapter Two

Here, There &
Now & Then

8 minutes, 22 seconds

The Beatles' longest track, 'Revolution 9' from *The Beatles* (also known as the *White Album*), is an experimental sound collage conceived by Lennon. Spanning over 8 minutes, the piece features a looped voice repeating the phrase "number nine" 12 times, contributing to its hypnotic and avant-garde feel. In stark contrast, the band's shortest track is McCartney's 'Her Majesty' from *Abbey Road* – a playful snippet lasting just 23 seconds.

〝We're not Beatles to each other, you know. It's a joke to us. If we're going out the door of the hotel, we don't say, 'Right! Beatle John! Beatle George now! Come on, let's go!' We don't put on a false front or anything. 〞

John Lennon, *Look*, December 1966

The iconic Beatles lineup finalized on 14 August 1962, when Ringo Starr agreed to join the band, replacing original drummer Pete Best. Both the other Beatles and producer George Martin had doubts about Best's drumming, and Starr had already filled in on occasion. Starr received the offer from manager Brian Epstein while performing with Rory Storm and the Hurricanes at a Butlin's holiday camp. "I didn't do anything to make it happen apart from saying 'Yes'," Ringo later recalled.

When Starr filled in on drums during a show at the Kaiserkeller club, it left a lasting impact: "Bang! He kicks in, and it was an 'Oh, my god' moment," McCartney said. "We're all looking at each other going, 'Yeah. This is it.'"

Ringo's first official performance as a Beatle came just days later, on 18 August 1962, at Hulme Hall in Birkenhead.

The Beatles #2: Ringo Starr

Ringo Starr's iconic left-hand drumming on a right-handed kit gave him a uniquely melodic, laid-back style that became essential to the Beatles' sound. Often overlooked, he was a true innovator. After 1965's *Help!*, Ringo was also the only Beatle to seriously pursue acting, starring in notable films such as *Candy* (1968), *The Magic Christian* (1969, with Peter Sellers) and *Caveman* (1981), where he met his second wife, Barbara Bach, the "Bond girl" from *The Spy Who Loved Me* (1977). Paul McCartney later told *Rolling Stone* in 2015: "There's this revisionist history that it was all John and Paul. But it was four corners of a square; it wouldn't have worked without one of the sides. Ringo was the right angle."

'Love Me Do'

On 5 October 1962, the world changed forever – the Beatles released their debut single 'Love Me Do', recorded at Abbey Road studios.

Primarily written by McCartney around 1958 during school truancy songwriting sessions with Lennon, the song went on to be released in three different versions, each featuring a different drummer. Ironically, Ringo Starr – just two weeks into the band at the time – didn't play drums on the commercial single. Producer George Martin, unsure about Ringo's early performance, brought in session drummer Andy White to record the official version.

Ringo later admitted, "I was devastated that George Martin had his doubts about me! He has apologized several times since, but it was devastating – I hated the bugger for years!"

To be fair, he'd only been in the band two weeks.

Favourite Albums

Over the years, each member of the Beatles
shared a different personal favourite among
their albums. Ringo Starr favoured *Abbey Road*.
George Harrison named *Rubber Soul*, explaining,
"Even at that time, I think that it was the best one
we made." Paul McCartney chose *Sgt. Pepper's
Lonely Hearts Club Band*, noting, "I had a lot to
do with it." As for John Lennon, he preferred the
White Album, saying, "I always preferred it to
all the other albums, the music is far superior."

Unbeaten Legacy

From 1962 to 1970, the Beatles dominated the world of music. In just eight years, they released 24 UK singles and 12 studio albums – a creative output that changed the course of popular culture. They are the best-selling band in history, with estimated global sales exceeding 600 million units worldwide.

To this day, they hold the record for the No. 1 albums on the US *Billboard* 200 chart (19) and the most No. 1 singles on the *Billboard* Hot 100 chart (20). In the UK, they've had more No. 1 albums (15) and singles (17) in the UK than any other act.

Beatlemania

Throughout this time, the world was gripped by Beatlemania – an unprecedented fan and media frenzy. The term "Beatlemania" first appeared in the British press in late 1963. It soon exploded globally, reaching fever pitch after the band's debut on the *The Ed Sullivan Show* in February 1964. Watched by a record-breaking 73 million Americans, the appearance catapulted the band into stratospheric fame.

Screaming crowds, crushed police barricades, lost privacy and obsessive fans created the blueprint for modern pop fandom. The intensity of it all eventually led the Beatles to stop touring altogether.

Asked once to define Beatlemania, Lennon quipped, "I'm not going to try. I'll leave it to the psychologists and let them get it wrong."

Ringoisms

Ringo Starr was beloved for his malapropisms – or Ringoisms – as the band affectionately called them. A malapropism is the mistaken use of a word in place of a similar-sounding one, often with an amusing effect. "Ringo would say things slightly wrong, like people do, but his were always wonderful, very lyrical," Lennon once said.

Some of Ringo's most iconic Ringoisms ended up as the titles of Beatles songs – including 'Hard Day's Night', 'Eight Days a Week' and 'Tomorrow Never Knows'.

\\We were just a band that made it very, very big, that's all. Our best work was never recorded. \\

John Lennon, *Rolling Stone***, December 1970**

Essential Album #4:
Beatles for Sale

1. 'No Reply'
2. 'I'm a Loser'
3. 'Baby's in Black'
4. 'Rock and Roll Music'
5. 'I'll Follow the Sun'
6. 'Mr Moonlight'
7. 'Kansas City/Hey-Hey-Hey-Hey!'
8. 'Eight Days a Week'
9. 'Words of Love'
10. 'Honey Don't'
11. 'Every Little Thing'
12. 'I Don't Want to Spoil the Party'
13. 'What You're Doing'
14. 'Everybody's Trying
   to Be My Baby'

The Beatles' fourth studio album, *Beatles for Sale*, was released on 4 December 1964, at the height of Beatlemania. The album is notable for several reasons:

• It marked a shift away from their signature clean-cut "mop-top" sound toward more introspective and downbeat tunes

• It introduced early signs of studio experimentation, including hints of guitar feedback and non-pop instrumentation

• It was their first album to show a clear influence from Bob Dylan's writing style

At the time of recording, the band was understandably exhausted – *A Hard Day's Night* had been released just two months prior – reflecting a pace that would be almost unthinkable today.

"The commotion doesn't bother us anymore. It's like working in a bell factory. After a while you get used to the bells."

Paul McCartney, *The Daily Telegraph*, 1964

The Beatles #3: Paul McCartney

Paul McCartney, the Beatles' legendary bassist, holds the distinction of being the most successful composer in music history. Beyond his groundbreaking work with the Beatles, he has sold over 100 million albums and 100 million singles with his solo work and with the band Wings.

His accolades are staggering: two inductions into the Rock and Roll Hall of Fame (with the Beatles in 1988 and as a solo artist in 1999), an Academy Award, a Primetime Emmy Award and 19 Grammy Awards. He was appointed a Member of the Order of the British Empire in 1965 and received a knighthood in 1997 for his contributions to music.

The Beatles

Essential Album #5:
Help!

1. 'Help!'
2. 'The Night Before'
3. 'You've Got to Hide Your Love Away'
4. 'I Need You'
5. 'Another Girl'
6. 'You're Going to Lose That Girl'
7. 'Ticket to Ride'
8. 'Act Naturally'
9. 'It's Only Love'
10. 'You Like Me Too Much'
11. 'Tell Me What You See'
12. 'I've Just Seen a Face'
13. 'Yesterday'
14. 'Dizzy Miss Lizzy'

Here, There & Now & Then

Released on 6 August 1965, the Beatles' fifth studio album – in just two years! – *Help!* marked a major sonic and cultural shift for the band. Often cited as the world's first true soundtrack album, it accompanied the film of the same name, which premiered a week prior.

Help! was also the first pop album to receive serious critical acclaim, earning a nomination for Album of the Year at the 1966 Grammy Awards – a pioneering achievement for a pop group at the time. It also signalled a change in the Beatles' creative process, heavily influenced by their growing cannabis use. "We were smoking marijuana for breakfast," Lennon told *Rolling Stone* in 1971. "Nobody could communicate
with us, because we were just all glazed eyes, giggling all the time."

And in a wonderfully Beatlesque twist, the album cover famously features the group with their arms positioned in flag semaphore – but instead of H.E.L.P., they actually spell out N.U.J.V.

Not exactly a cry for help!

Total Chaos & Cheeky Wit

When the Beatles landed in New York in February 1964 for their US debut, Beatlemania crossed the Atlantic in full swing. At their first press conference at JFK Airport, the Fab Four faced a room full of sceptical American journalists who hurled a barrage of questions – many of them bizarre, loaded, or simply out of touch. But rather than taking offence, the Beatles answered with irresistible Scouse humour, unflappable charm and lightning-fast wit. These moments instantly became legend and cemented their reputation not just as musicians, but as cultural firecrackers.

"Two feet, nine inches!"
Ringo Starr, when asked how tall he is.

"No, we don't mind. We've got the records at home."
John Lennon, when asked if he was bothered the band couldn't hear themselves sing at concerts.

"We're not."
George Harrison, when asked about the criticism that they're not very good.

"Come and have a feel."
John Lennon, when asked "Are you for real?"

"When I feel my head start to swell, I look at Ringo and know perfectly well we're not supermen."
John Lennon, when asked by press if adulation from teenage girls affects him.

"Anytime you spell Beetle with an 'a' in it, we get the money."
Ringo Starr, on the litany of Beatles merch

Hello, America

As he first stepped off the plane at New York's Kennedy Airport on 7 February 1964 for the Beatles' first visit to the US, Ringo Starr exclaimed, "So, this is America. They must be out of their minds!"

Greeted by 5,000 screaming fans, it was the explosive beginning of Beatlemania in America. "We knew that America would make us or break us as world stars," manager Brian Epstein told Pop Chronicles 1964. "In fact, she made us."

Just two days later, the Beatles made their momentous debut on *The Ed Sullivan Show* –and the rest, as they say, is history ...

Viva Las Beatles

On 20 August 1964, the Beatles played their one and only Las Vegas show – a sold-out, 29-minute set for over 17,000 screaming fans at the now-iconic Convention Centre.

Confined to Suite 2344 at the Sahara Hotel due to thousands of desperate fans eager to see them, two slot machines were brought up to the Beatles' room to pass the time. It was the band's first attempt at gambling – they didn't win a thing, but they did leave Vegas £33,000 richer (equivalent to more than £800,000 today) for half an hour's work. Not bad!

Famous Fans

As the most influential musical group of all time, it goes without saying that the Beatles have picked up a few famous fans…

"The Beatles were doing things nobody was doing. Their chords were outrageous, and their harmonies made it all valid. They were pointing the direction of where music had to go."
Bob Dylan, *Rolling Stone*, 2014

"The Beatles are just a phenomenon; everything that the people say they are, they are. They're great… Their music is just melodious."
Little Richard, *Pop Chronicles*, 1968

"If it weren't for the Beatles, I would not be a musician."
Dave Grohl, *NME*, July 2012

"The Beatles were so big that it's hard for people not alive at the time to realize just how big they were. There isn't a real comparison with anyone now. They were so big that to be competitive with them was impossible. I'm talking about in record sales and tours and all this. They were huge."
Mick Jagger, *Rolling Stone*, December 1995

"I declare that the Beatles are mutants. Prototypes of evolutionary agents sent by God, endowed with a mysterious power to create a new human species, a young race of laughing freemen."
Timothy Leary, *Shout!*, 1981

"The Beatles came from a very similar background – the industrial towns in England, working class; they wrote their own songs, conquered the world. That was the blueprint for lots of other British kids to try to do the same."
Sting, *The Guardian*, 2000

Essential Album #6.1:
Rubber Soul (UK)

1. 'Drive My Car'
2. 'Norwegian Wood (This Bird Has Flown)'
3. 'You Won't See Me'
4. 'Nowhere Man'
5. 'Think for Yourself'
6. 'The Word'
7. 'Michelle'
8. 'What Goes On'
9. 'Girl'
10. 'I'm Looking Through You'
11. 'In My Life'
12. 'Wait'
13. 'If I Needed Someone'
14. 'Run for Your Life'

Perhaps the most quintessentially "Beatles" Beatles album, *Rubber Soul* marked yet another artistic turning point when it was released on 3 December 1965. The band shifted gears from upbeat pop toward a more introspective folk-rock sound, redefining what pop music could be – again.

The album's title came from a phrase McCartney overheard describing Mick Jagger's vocal style – "plastic soul", a nod to both cheeky and self-aware.

Among many standout tracks, 'In My Life' remains a fan and critic favourite – and perhaps the most debated song in the Beatles' catalogue. It's the only Lennon–McCartney composition where even the songwriters themselves and Beatles scholars alike continue to disagree on who wrote what.

The now-legendary 2004 edition of Rolling Stone's "500 Greatest Songs of All Time" list included 23 Beatles songs (more than any other musical act on the list) – a clear indication of the group's essential importance in rock and roll history:

Here, There & Now & Then

Essential Album #6.2:
Rubber Soul (US)

1. 'I've Just Seen a Face'

2. 'Norwegian Wood (This Bird Has Flown)'

3. 'You Won't See Me'

4. 'Think for Yourself'

5. 'The Word'

6. 'Michelle'

7. 'It's Only Love'

8. 'Girl'

9. 'I'm Looking Through You'

10. 'In My Life'

11. 'Wait'

12. 'Run for Your Life'

When *Rubber Soul* was released in the US just three days later, it arrived as a slightly different album – literally. Capitol Records trimmed the original UK tracklist, omitting songs like 'Drive My Car' and adding 'I've Just Seen a Face' and 'It's Only Love', giving the US version a more acoustic, folk-driven feel. Whether by accident or design, it aligned perfectly with the American folk-rock movement gaining momentum at the time.

The result was an album that resonated deeply with US listeners and critics alike, offering a more introspective, lyrically mature Beatles than many had heard before. The shift in tone marked a major turning point –not just in the band'ssound, but in how pop music was perceived. Suddenly, albums weren't just a collection of hits; they were cohesive artistic statements.

Chapter Three

*Magic &
Mystery*

\\ Paul and I wrote a lot of stuff together, one-on-one, eyeball to eyeball. Like in 'I Want to Hold Your Hand', I remember when we got the chord that made the song. We were in Jane Asher's house, downstairs in the cellar playing on the piano at the same time. And we had, 'Oh you-u-u... got that something...' And Paul hits this chord, and I turn to him and say, 'That's it!' I said, 'Do that again!' In those days, we really used to absolutely write like that – both playing into each other's nose. \\

John Lennon, *Playboy*, January 1981

Lennon–McCartney

The most successful – and most influential – songwriting partnership in musical history belongs to John Lennon and Paul McCartney. Between 1962 and 1969, the duo co-wrote approximately 180 songs, with 60 of them charting on the US *Billboard* Hot 100 – including 20 No. 1 hits, more than any other musical act. "We both had our fingers in each other's pies," Lennon once said in *Rolling Stone*, December 1970.

Their legendary partnership was never formalized with a legal contract. "Paul and I made a deal when we were 15," Lennon told *Playboy* in September 1980. "There was never a legal deal between us, just a deal we made when we decided to write together that we put both our names on it, no matter what."

That handshake agreement would go on to generate a catalogue worth several billion pounds – and change popular music forever.

Magical Mystery Tour

Often considered the only misstep in the Beatles' otherwise flawless career, *Magical Mystery Tour* was a surreal and experimental television film that aired on the BBC on Boxing Day, 1967 – and it was met with critical disaster.

Conceived and largely directed by Paul McCartney, the film follows the band on a psychedelic bus journey through the English countryside, joined by a cast of eccentric characters including Happy Nat the Rubber Man and Buster Bloodvessel. With no clear plot, the 60-minute film is a chaotic mix of comedy skits and musical performances, featuring songs like 'I Am the Walrus', 'The Fool on the Hill' and 'Your Mother Should Know'.

Today, the film stands as a curious snapshot of the Beatles' psychedelic phase and a reflection of their creative uncertainty following the death of their manager Brian Epstein. Responding to the backlash, McCartney asked, with a touch of humour: "Was the film really all that bad compared to the rest of Christmas TV?" Fair point.

Psychedelia

In the mid-1960s, the Beatles became the first major rock group to popularize psychedelia and its surreal soundscapes and spiritual undertones. Their journey began unexpectedly in March 1965, when Lennon and Harrison were unknowingly dosed with LSD by their dentist, who spiked their coffee during a dinner party.

The experience opened new dimensions of creativity. Albums like *Revolver*, *Sgt. Pepper's Lonely Hearts Club Band* and *Magical Mystery Tour* heavily feature experimental sounds, tape loops and abstract lyrics – all shaped by the band's mind-expanding trips. At one point, the group were taking LSD so regularly that Lennon later admitted, "We did think we were going barmy!"

\\ **For all our success, the Beatles were always a great little band. Nothing more, nothing less.** \\

Paul McCartney, *Tampa Bay Times*, 2000

Lost Fortune

Had the Beatles signed modern contracts and replicated their 1960s success today, they would have earned over £3.5 billion from sales, merchandise and publishing. Instead, they made relatively little due to notoriously unfair early agreements. Their 1962 EMI contract paid just one British penny per single – split four ways. A 1963 merchandising deal gave them a mere 10 per cent of proceeds, losing them an estimated $100 million – approximately $1 billion in today's money.

"On paper we're very wealthy people. Just when it gets down to pound notes, we're only half wealthy," Ringo said in *Scene and Heard* in January 1969. By the time they split, the four members had less than $2 million between them, a stark contrast to the vast fortune they generated for others.

Apple Corps

In 1968, the Beatles launched Apple Corps – an ambitious multimedia corporation, envisioned as a creative hub for music, film and art. The company embodied the band's creative spirit, if not their business acumen.

Years later, in a tribute to the band he adored, Steve Jobs named his startup Apple Computers – a deliberate move away from the technical-sounding names dominating the 1970s tech industry. "My model for business is the Beatles," Jobs once said. "They were four guys who kept each other's kind of negative tendencies in check. They balanced each other and the total was greater than the sum of the parts. That's how I see business."

Today, Apple, Inc. stands as the world's first trillion-dollar business – a testament, in part, to the creative inspiration sparked by four lads from Liverpool.

\\ We're in the happy position of not really needing any more money. So, for the first time, the bosses aren't in it for profit. If you come and see me and say, 'I've had such and such a dream', I'll say, 'Here's so much money. Go away and do it.' We've already bought all our dreams. So now we want to share that possibility with others. \\

Paul McCartney, Apple Press Conference,
11 May 1968

Turning Awfully Funny

By October 1967, the Beatles' transformation was pretty much complete. No longer the squeaky-clean "Fab Four", they had fully embraced psychedelia – a far cry from their mop-top beginnings. Amid this radical shift, Queen Elizabeth II hosted an event at Buckingham Palace, where she reportedly turned to Sir Joseph Lockwood, chairman of EMI, and commented: "The Beatles are turning awfully funny, aren't they?" Her remark perfectly captured the establishment's quiet confusion at the radical cultural shifts the Beatles were spearheading – a band evolving far beyond pop fame into the heart of the Sixties counterculture revolution.

The Greatest Gig Ever

From 1958 to 1969, the Beatles performed more than 1,400 live shows – an astonishing number, especially as they stopped touring in 1966.

One of their most iconic gigs was the *NME* Annual Poll-Winners' All-Star Concert on 1 May 1966, at London's Empire Pool in Wembley. Often dubbed as the "greatest gig ever", the event featured a legendary lineup: the Rolling Stones, the Who, Dusty Springfield, the Yardbirds, the Walker Brothers, Roy Orbison, Cliff Richard, the Shadows, Herman's Hermits and the Small Faces. Each performed short sets of their biggest hits to 10,000 screaming fans.

It was also a milestone: the last time the Beatles played live before a British audience again, save for their one-off performance on the rooftop of Apple Corps HQ on 30 January 1969.

Shea Stadium Setlist

1. 'Twist and Shout'

2. 'She's a Woman'

3. 'I Feel Fine'

4. 'Dizzy Miss Lizzy'

5. 'Ticket to Ride'

6. 'Everybody's Trying to Be My Baby'

7. 'Can't Buy Me Love'

8. 'Baby's in Black'

9. 'Act Naturally'

10. 'A Hard Day's Night'

11. 'Help!'

12. 'I'm Down'

On 15 August 1965, the Beatles played at Shea
Stadium, New York – a defining moment in
music history and the height of Beatlemania.
Performing to a record-shattering crowd of
55,600 screaming fans, it was the first stadium
rock concert ever, and the first time a sports
stadium hosted a large-scale entertainment
event. The deafening screams were so intense
that Ringo Starr couldn't hear a thing, relying
instead on visual cues – John Lennon's head
bobbing or Paul McCartney's foot tapping –
to keep the beat. At one point, McCartney joked
to the roaring crowd, "It's loud, isn't it?!"

Also in the crowd that day? Linda Eastman and
Barbara Bach – two women who, unbeknownst
to anyone back then, would one day marry Paul
and Ringo.

\\ **Beatles are really the only people who can play Beatle music.** \\

John Lennon, *Flip*, May 1966

Royal Variety Show 1963

With the now-iconic quip, "For our last number, I'd like to ask your help. Would the people in the cheaper seats clap your hands. And the rest of you, if you'll just rattle your jewellery," John Lennon cheekily signed off the Beatles' four-song set at the Royal Variety Performance on 4 November 1963. The band performed 'From Me to You', 'She Loves You', 'Till There Was You' and 'Twist and Shout' to an audience that included the highest-ranking members of the Royal Family: Queen Elizabeth II, the Queen Mother and Princess Margaret.

Before the show, Lennon had reportedly told manager Brian Epstein that he intended to say, "Rattle your *fuckin'* jewellery," but, to Epstein's relief, he toned it down at the last moment – though the cheeky charm remained unmistakably Lennon.

The Butcher Cover

The June 1966 release of US album *Yesterday and Today* is infamous for its original "Butcher Cover". This controversial image depicted the band in white butcher coats surrounded by raw meat and dismembered doll parts! Photographer Robert Whitaker intended it to be pop art commentary on the band's fame and a statement against the Vietnam War. The gruesome imagery caused immediate outrage, except with the band. "It didn't seem offensive to us," McCartney said in *The Beatles Anthology*, 1995. "It was more original than what most other photographers asked us to do."

Capitol Records swiftly recalled the album. The withdrawn "Butcher Cover" LPs have since become valuable collectors' items. Lennon's personal, signed copy sold for a record-breaking £180,000 ($234,400)!

"We turn into Beatles because everybody looking at us sees the Beatles. We're not the Beatles at all. We're just us."

John Lennon, *Look*, December 1966

Essential Album #7:
Revolver

1. 'Taxman'
2. 'Eleanor Rigby'
3. 'I'm Only Sleeping'
4. 'Love You To'
5. 'Here, There and Everywhere'
6. 'Yellow Submarine'
7. 'She Said She Said'
8. 'Good Day Sunshine'
9. 'And Your Bird Can Sing'
10. 'For No One'
11. 'Doctor Robert'
12. 'I Want to Tell You'
13. 'Got to Get You Into My Life'
14. 'Tomorrow Never Knows'

Often regarded as the Beatles' greatest album, *Revolver* was released on 5 August 1966 – just five days after England's legendary FIFA World Cup win. A true masterpiece of studio innovation, *Revolver* marked the band's leap into psychedelia, with groundbreaking tracks like 'Eleanor Rigby' and the mind-bending 'Tomorrow Never Knows' (the famous high-pitched bird-like sound at the start of 'Tomorrow Never Knows' is actually McCartney's laugh, sped up and distorted).

"There are sounds on *Revolver* that nobody else has done yet – I mean nobody... *ever*," Paul McCartney said in a 1966 interview. Remarkably, none of the songs from this era-defining album were ever performed live by the band. The title itself was a late decision – a pun on how LP (long play) records spin at 33.3 revolutions per minute. Lennon had jokingly suggested calling the album "Four Sides of the Eternal Triangle".

The Three Phases of the Beatles' Ten-Year Tenure at the Top:

1. *The Beatlemania Era* **(1962–1964)**
Defined by their clean-cut mop-top charm and the deafening screams of teenage fans, this era saw the release of albums that propelled them from Liverpool lads to global superstars.

2. *The Bob Dylan Revolution* **(1965–1967)**
Arguably their creative peak, this phase was shaped by Bob Dylan's influence, psychedelic experimentation and a full embrace of counterculture. The result? Sonic revolutions with kaleidoscopic flair.

3. *The Bearded Era* **(1968–1970)**
The Beatles traded mop tops for moustaches and harmony for heaviness, and this era was marked by introspection, raw rock energy and visible signs of the band's looming breakup – not least their ever-present facial hair.

"We were lucky that there were four of us to take the pressure. We've all said this about Elvis: he was on his own. The four of us held each other together. At certain times, each one of us went mad, but the other three could bring us back."

Ringo Starr, *The Beatles Anthology*, November 1995

Controversial Comments

In March 1966, John Lennon ignited a massive uproar in the US with his controversial remark: "The Beatles are more popular than Jesus." Made during an interview with the *Evening Standard*, the comment caused little stir in the UK but ignited outrage across America's Bible Belt. Radio stations banned Beatles songs, and fans staged "Beatles burnings" of records and merchandise. Under mounting pressure, Lennon issued a reluctant apology at a press conference, where he also famously added, "If I'd said television was bigger than Jesus, I might have gotten away with it."

\\ I'd hate the Beatles to be remembered as four jovial mop tops – four silly little puppets, which is what Americans tend to think of us sometimes. If it's possible, I'd like us to be remembered, when we're dead, as four people who made music that stands up to being remembered. \\

Paul McCartney, *Disc and Music Echo*, June 1966

Essential Album #8

Sgt. Pepper's Lonely Hearts Club Band

1. 'Sgt. Pepper's Lonely Hearts Club Band'
2. 'With a Little Help from My Friends'
3. 'Lucy in the Sky with Diamonds'
4. 'Getting Better'
5. 'Fixing a Hole'
6. 'She's Leaving Home'
7. 'Being for the Benefit of Mr Kite!'
8. 'Within you Without You'
9. 'When I'm Sixty-Four'
10. 'Lovely Rita'
11. 'Good Morning Good Morning'
12. 'Sgt. Pepper's Lonely Hearts Club Band (Reprise)'
13. 'A Day in the Life'

Released on 1 June 1967, *Sgt. Pepper's Lonely Hearts Club Band* is widely considered the Beatles' most revolutionary work. It popularized the concept album, was the first pop record mastered without gaps between tracks for a continuous live feel, and featured the era's most expensive cover art – costing £2,868 (around £38,823 today!), 100 times more than the average.

The iconic title stemmed from McCartney's desire to escape the constraints of Beatle identity. As he explained in 1967: "We were fed up with being Beatles. We were not boys, we were men... Let's develop alter egos so we're not having to project an image which we know. It would be much more free."

❯❯ I thought we were the best fucking group in the goddamn world and believing that is what made us what we were... As far as we were concerned, we were the best, but we thought we were the best before anybody else had even heard of us... So, in that respect I think the Beatles are the best thing that ever happened in pop music, but you play me those tracks, and I want to remake every damn one of them. ❯❯

John Lennon, *Playboy*, September 1980

Laughter & Nirvana

On 28 August 1964, at New York's Delmonico Hotel, the Beatles were first introduced to their burgeoning folk hero, Bob Dylan. That night, Dylan famously introduced the band to marijuana. Ringo, inexperienced with cannabis, reportedly smoked the entire joint and collapsed into uncontrollable giggles. McCartney, meanwhile, became so high he believed he'd reached enlightenment, asking the band's roadie Mal Evans to document his revelations. The next morning, Evans handed McCartney a note that read simply: "There are seven levels." Dylan, equally stoned, allegedly called the hotel reception declaring, "This is Beatlemania here!"

On-Screen Stars

In November 2021, *The Lord of the Rings* director Peter Jackson released *Get Back* on Disney+. This three-part docuseries re-examined the Beatles' *Let It Be* sessions using 60 hours of unseen footage and 150 hours of unheard audio. Long thought to be defined by tension, the sessions were revealed to be far more joyful and collaborative. One standout moment shows Paul McCartney spontaneously crafting the melody for 'Get Back' in real time.

While never considered cinematic masterpieces, the Beatles did star – and genuinely act! – in two popular movies: *A Hard Day's Night* (1964) and *Help!* (1965). The former follows 36 chaotic hours of Beatlemania as the band dodges fans and prepares for a live TV performance. In *Help!*, the plot takes a surreal turn as Ringo is pursued by a sinister Eastern cult after a sacrificial ring becomes stuck on his finger. Both films are packed with zany antics and sharp one-liners that perfectly capture the band's signature Scouse wit.

"**The Beatles were just four guys that loved each other. That's all they'll ever be.**"

Ringo Starr, *The Beatles Anthology*, November 1995

Chapter Four

The Fab Four

29 August 1966

The date the Beatles played their final official concert at Candlestick Park, home of the San Francisco Giants baseball team. They performed 11 songs, closing with 'Long Tall Sally'. In the wake of Lennon's "more popular than Jesus" remark, the 42,000-capacity show was only half-full. The band, clearly exhausted and fed up with the chaotic screaming, were keen to quit touring. Sensing the end, George Harrison reportedly turned to the others on the flight back home and said, "That's it, then, I'm not a Beatle anymore."

\\ **The Beatles saved the world from boredom. We were just a little band from Liverpool. It wasn't that we were important. We were just different.** \\

George Harrison, *The Beatles Anthology*, November 1995

Essential Album #9:

The Beatles
(the White Album)

1. 'Back in the U.S.S.R.'
2. 'Dear Prudence'
3. 'Glass Onion'
4. 'Ob-La-Di, Ob-La-Da'
5. 'Wild Honey Pie'
6. 'The Continuing Story
   of Bungalow Bill'
7. 'While My Guitar
   Gently Weeps'
8. 'Happiness Is a Warm Gun'
9. 'Martha My Dear'
10. 'I'm So Tired'
11. 'Blackbird'
12. 'Piggies'
13. 'Rocky Raccoon'
14. 'Don't Pass Me By'
15. 'Why Don't We Do
    It in the Road?'

16. 'I Will'
17. 'Julia'
18. 'Birthday'
19. 'Yer Blues'
20. 'Mother Nature's Son'
21. 'Everybody's Got
    Something to Hide Except
    Me and My Monkey'
22. 'Sexy Sadie'
23. 'Helter Skelter'
24. 'Long, Long, Long'
25. 'Revolution 1'
26. 'Honey Pie'
27. 'Savoy Truffle'
28. 'Cry Baby Cry'
29. 'Revolution 9'
30. 'Good Night'

More commonly known as the *White Album*, *The Beatles* – a 30-track double album released in November 1968 – starkly revealed the band's diverging songwriting paths and growing tensions. Only 16 of the 30 tracks feature all four members performing together.

Its minimalist cover, a plain white sleeve embossed with the band's name, stood in stark contrast to *Sgt Pepper*'s colourful chaos and symbolized a desire to return "back to basics". Tensions ran so high during the sessions that Ringo famously (and briefly) quit the band. Lennon later reflected: "The break-up of the Beatles can be heard on that album."

A Prestigious Honour

On 26 October 1965, the Beatles
were appointed Members of the Order
of the British Empire (MBE) by Queen
Elizabeth II – the first pop/rock musicians
to receive such a prestigious and
traditionally conservative honour.
The decision caused a stir among the
British establishment, with some former
recipients even returning their medals in
protest. Four years later, John Lennon did
the same – but for very different reasons.
In November 1969, he sent back his MBE
with a note that read: "Your Majesty, I am
returning my MBE as a protest against
Britain's involvement in the Nigeria-Biafra
thing, against our support of America
in Vietnam and against 'Cold Turkey'
slipping down the charts."
Always the joker!

'Strawberry Fields Forever' / 'Penny Lane'

Often hailed as the greatest double A-side single ever released, 'Strawberry Fields Forever'/'Penny Lane' hit the shelves on 13 February 1967. Both songs are steeped in Liverpool nostalgia, drawn from places Lennon and McCartney loved as kids. The release marked a turning point in the Beatles' sound, showcasing their psychedelic evolution and contrasting styles: Lennon's introspective dreamscape in 'Strawberry Fields Forever' and McCartney's bright, melodic charm in 'Penny Lane'.

Lennon later called 'Strawberry Fields Forever' his finest Beatles' work, while McCartney recalled: "On the bus to John's house to write songs, I'd have to change at Penny Lane, so we often hung out at that terminus, like a roundabout."

25 June 1967

Etched in cultural history, this day marked the Beatles' performance of "All You Need Is Love" during *Our World* – the first-ever live global television broadcast! Beamed to an estimated 400 million viewers across five continents, the performance from Olympic Studios in London wasn't just a musical event – it was a powerful moment of unity and a bold, anti-war statement during the famed "Summer of Love".

With their shift into kaleidoscopic psychedelia on full display, the Beatles embodies the spirit of Swinging London at its most idealistic. As John Lennon told the BBC that day: "It was for love and bloody peace, and we were big enough to command an audience of that size."

The Beatles #4: George Harrison

The quiet one, George Harrison was also the youngest Beatle. Come the group's demise, Harrison had quietly emerged as one of their greatest assets – a gifted guitarist and songwriter in his own right. Frank Sinatra famously commented on his ballad 'Something', calling it "one of the best love songs I believe to be written in the past fifty or a hundred years".

After the Beatles, Harrison's solo career was peppered with surprises: he helped form the chart-topping supergroup the Travelling Wilburys and famously bankrolled two of Britain's greatest comedy films – *Monty Python's Life of Brian* (1979) and *Withnail & I* (1987).

Essential Album #10:
Yellow Submarine

1. 'Yellow Submarine'
2. 'Only a Northern Song'
3. 'All Together Now'
4. 'Hey Bulldog'
5. 'It's All Too Much'
6. 'All You Need Is Love'
7. 'Pepperland'
8. 'Sea of Time'
9. 'Sea of Holes'
10. 'Sea of Monsters'
11. 'March of the Meanies'
12. 'Pepperland Laid Waste'
13. 'Yellow Submarine
    in Pepperland'

So quipped Paul McCartney in 1968, referring to *Yellow Submarine*, the groundbreaking animated film whose soundtrack album was released in January 1969. The album featured six previously unreleased Beatles tracks, alongside orchestral pieces composed by George Martin.

In the film, the animated Beatles journey in a yellow submarine to Pepperland, a musical paradise invaded by the nefarious Blue Meanies. Through song and love, they restore peace, colour and harmony to Pepperland. Bizarrely, none of the Beatles voiced their own animated characters – though they appear in a live-action cameo, where Lennon famously signs off: "There's only one way to go out… singing!"

"Paul is Dead"

In December 1969, wild rumours began circulating that Paul McCartney had died in a 1966 moped accident and had been secretly replaced by a look-alike. The bizarre "Paul is Dead" conspiracy theory took hold, prompting fans to scour Beatles songs and album covers for supposed "clues" – like McCartney's bare feet on *Abbey Road*, or hidden meaning in lyrics. McCartney eventually addressed the speculated, joking, "I am fit as a fiddle. I am alive and well and concerned about the rumours of my death. But if I were dead, I would be the last to know."

Despite the obvious absurdity, the theory became a significant pop culture myth, with many still adding to its legend today.

"There's an old joke, but it's true: sometimes you'd get this girl after a show, and you'd be in bed, and she'd ask you which Beatle you are. I'd say, 'Which one do you like?' If she said, 'George,' I'd say, 'I'm George'."

John Lennon, *Los Angeles Times*, November 1980

Merch Madness

During the peak of Beatlemania (1963–1966), Beatles-themed merchandise exploded. Beyond the expected wigs, lunchboxes and doormats, the market was flooded with bizarre items, including Ringo Starr bubble bath dolls, Beatles talcum powder, insect-repellent mothballs and even nylon stockings. At one point, even one of Lennon's extracted teeth became a collectible.

"I think everyone has gone daft!" Lennon said in 1964 of the mania surrounding Beatles merchandise.

In that year alone, licensed Beatles products grossed an astonishing $50 million in the US – roughly $500,000 million today. Almost none of it went to the Beatles themselves.

One Last Gig

The Beatles' iconic rooftop gig took place on 30 January 1969, atop the Apple Corps building in central London. They performed five songs – 'Get Back', 'Don't Let Me Down', 'I've Got a Feeling', 'One After 909' and 'Dig a Pony' – several times before police pulled the plug. Down on Savile Row, hundreds of fans stopped to listen.

The band had initially considered more extravagant venues for their final performance – including a Roman amphitheatre in Tunisia or even a cruise ship – but, as Ringo later said, "We would have had to take all the stuff…so we decided, 'Let's get up on the roof'."

Before the police intervened, Lennon got the last word: "I'd like to say, 'thank you' on behalf of the group and ourselves, and I hope we passed the audition." The Beatles never performed together again.

Essential Album #11

Abbey Road

1. 'Come Together'
2. 'Something'
3. 'Maxwell's Silver Hammer'
4. 'Oh! Darling'
5. 'Octopus's Garden'
6. 'I Want You (She's So Heavy)'
7. 'Here Comes the Sun'
8. 'Because'
9. 'You Never Give Me Your Money'
10. 'Sun King'
11. 'Mean Mr Mustard'
12. 'Polythene Pam'
13. 'She Came in Through the Bathroom Window'
14. 'Golden Slumbers'
15. 'Carry That Weight'
16. 'The End'
17. 'Her Majesty'

The Fab Four

Released in September 1969, *Abbey Road* was the final album the Beatles recorded together. Though reviews were mixed at first, it's now considered a masterpiece. Its iconic cover – showing the band on the zebra crossing outside EMI Studios – featured neither the band's name nor album title. Designer John Kosh famously told EMI, "We didn't need to write the band's name on the cover... They were the most famous band in the world." Eagle-eyed fans also noticed a white Volkswagen Beetle in the shot. Its number plate (LMW 281F) became so iconic it was repeatedly stolen, much to the owner's anguish.

The Near Reunion

After their split in 1970, the Beatles received countless multi-million-dollar offers to reunite – but they never did. Still, they came surprisingly close. On 24 April 1976, during a live episode of *Saturday Night Live,* producer Lorne Michaels famously made a live, on-air offer of $3,000 to the Beatles to appear on the show and play three songs. In an incredible twist of fate, Lennon and McCartney happened to be together that night at Lennon's New York apartment – just 22 blocks from the studio – watching the show live. The pair reportedly laughed and briefly considered hopping in a cab and surprising the audience, but ultimately decided against it. It remains one of music's greatest *what if* moments.

The Mystery Oscar

Despite their relatively short career, The Beatles amassed an impressive number of awards – from 8 Grammys and 4 BRITs to numerous Ivor Novellos. Perhaps the most unexpected accolade they ever won was an Academy Award for Best Original Song Score for the film *Let It Be* in 1971.

Before the ceremony, super-producer, and the Academy Award's musical director, Quincy Jones tried to convince McCartney that the band might win and that they should attend, but he wasn't interested. Jones accepted the Oscar on their behalf, saying: "I wish the Beatles were all here together tonight to receive this, but on their behalf, thank you very much!" Today, the location of the Beatles' Oscar remains a mystery.

The Beginning of the End

John Lennon was tragically murdered on 8 December 1980, outside his home in New York City. His final reported words were "I'm shot", after deranged gunman Mark Chapman fired four bullets into his back with a .38 Special revolver. Just hours earlier, Lennon had given a hopeful interview to RKO Radio, saying: "I've always considered my work one piece, and I consider that my work won't be finished until I am dead and buried and I hope that's a long, long time."

The Beatles Anthology

In 1995, the three surviving Beatles – McCartney, Harrison and Starr – reunited for the first and only time to create *The Beatles Anthology*, a landmark documentary chronicling the band's history. As part of the project, they recorded new instrumental and vocal parts for two of John Lennon's unfinished demos: "Free As A Bird" and "Real Love", both of which went on to become global No. 1 singles.

Reflecting on the band's enduring legacy, George Harrison captured it perfectly: "The Beatles will just go on and on – our records and films and videos and books, and in people's memories and minds, has become its own thing now. The Beatles exist without us."

Essential Album #12:
Let It Be

1. 'Two of Us'
2. 'Dig a Pony'
3. 'Across the Universe'
4. 'I Me Mine'
5. 'Dig It'
6. 'Let It Be'
7. 'Maggie Mae'
8. 'I've Got a Feeling'
9. 'One After 909'
10. 'The Long and Winding Road'
11. 'For You Blue'
12. 'Get Back'

Released in May 1970, *Let It Be* arrived after the Beatles had already broken up – yet it was actually recorded before *Abbey Road*. The album includes timeless tracks like 'Two of Us', 'Let It Be', 'Get Back' and 'The Long and Winding Road'. Frustrations ran high during production, especially when John Lennon brought in producer Phil Spector to rework the material – or as McCartney put it, "overproduce it".

The album's title came from a dream McCartney had about his late mother, Mary, who had passed away when he was 14. In the dream, she comforted him with the words, "It's gonna be alright. Just let it be" – a message that stayed with him during the band's stormy final chapter.

The Beatles #5: George Martin

The title of "Fifth Beatle" supposedly belongs to the band's visionary producer, George Martin. It was Martin who transformed Lennon and McCartney's raw songs into polished masterpieces, shaping their sound, arranging their music and pushing the limits of what a studio could do. Despite being 36 when he first met the group – 16 years their senior – Martin affectionately referred to the band members as his "little brothers".

"They astonished me with their ideas," he once remarked. "Each song was a gem, and I said to myself, 'It can't last.' I'd say to them, 'That's great, now give me a better one.' And they did." Without Martin, the Beatles' catalogue may never have seen the light of day.

As if bridging the old and new, Martin introduced himself after the first session by saying, "If there's anything you don't like, let me know." George Harrison famously replied, "Well, I don't like your tie for a start."

" Somebody said to me, 'But the Beatles were anti-materialistic.' That's a huge myth. John and I literally used to sit down and say, 'Now let's write a swimming pool.' We said it out of innocence. Out of normal, fucking working-class glee that we were able to write a 'swimming pool'. For the first time in our lives, we could actually do something and earn money. "

Paul McCartney, *Rolling Stone*, February 1990

Funny Frequencies

After the monumental E-major piano chord
that closes 'A Day in the Life', UK vinyl pressings
of 1967's *Sgt. Pepper's Lonely Hearts Club Band*
featured two delightful auditory surprises.
At John Lennon's suggestion, a 15-kilohertz
high-frequency tone – inaudible to humans but
sure to irritate dogs – was embedded in the
groove. This was followed by an endless loop
of surreal laughter and gibberish, cut into
the run-out groove. On older turntables,
the needle would spin indefinitely, trapping
listeners (and their poor dogs) in a perpetual
loop of Beatlemania absurdity. Just another
day in the life of the Beatles!

20 January 1988

The date the Beatles were inducted into the prestigious Rock and Roll Hall of Fame. George Harrison and Ringo Starr attended the ceremony, while Paul McCartney declined due to ongoing business disputes.

Rolling Stones frontman Mick Jagger gave the induction speech, reflecting: "We went through some pretty strange times together but they were the greatest times of our lives." Harrison's speech stole the show with its dry humour. "The Beatles have gotten a bit bigger than any of us expected, but it's certainly wonderful to be here and certainly a thrill. Blame Little Richard, it's all his fault really."

Everything Else Can Wait…

George Harrison died on 29 November 2001, at 58, following a long battle with lung cancer. His final words to his family – "Everything else can wait, but the search for God cannot wait… love one another" – beautifully encapsulated his sweet, spiritual nature.

His premature death might not have happened had intruder Michael Abram, two years prior, not brutally attacked Harrison and his wife Olivia at their home. Abram, a paranoid schizophrenic, stabbed Harrison multiple times, puncturing a lung. Olivia bravely fought him off, striking him with a fireplace poker and lamp, which allowed them to subdue him until police arrived. While Harrison survived the assault, it's believed it contributed to his subsequent lung problems that later took his life.

Going Back in Time

In April 2028, acclaimed Oscar-winning director Sir Sam Mendes will release four separate films about the Beatles – each one telling the band's rise to superstardom from the perspective of a different member. Described as the most ambitious and innovative musical biopic ever made, the four interconnected stories will each have a unique theatrical release and are designed to "sync up" when viewed as a whole.

Filmed over 15 months – with each film shot over a three-month period – the project features a stellar cast: Harris Dickinson as John Lennon, Paul Mescal as Paul McCartney, Joseph Quinn as George Harrison and Barry Keoghan as Ringo Starr. "I am honoured to be telling the story of the greatest rock band of all time," Mendes said, when announcing the project in February 2024.

\\ **Life is an energy field,
a bunch of molecules. And
these particular molecules
formed to make these
four guys, the Beatles...
I have to think that was
something metaphysical.
Something alchemic.
Something that must be
thought of as magic.** \\

Paul McCartney, *Newsweek*, March 1982